CW00404374

Lisieux

A Pilgrim's Companion

by
David Baldwin

To young people - our hope and our future

*All booklets are published thanks to the
generous support of the members of the
Catholic Truth Society*

CATHOLIC TRUTH SOCIETY
PUBLISHERS TO THE HOLY SEE

Contents

Thérèse's Lisieux

Lisieux is a small, charming, rural town in Normandy of some 27,000 souls, set in a valley at the confluence of the rivers Touques and Orbiquet. It is a commune in the Calvados departement of Basse-Normandie, and is the capital town of the communities of Pays d'Auge. It is close to the coastal holiday resorts of Côte Fleurie, and is about an hour's drive from each of the cross Channel ferry ports of Le Havre and Caen. The gentle rolling countryside is very reminiscent of rural, farming England, and the area is well known for its smooth Calvados, handsome châteaux and tasty cheese! It is twinned with Taunton, in Somerset – an area also known for its apple and dairy products, and stately homes. On the suburban outskirts of Taunton there is the small, charming Parish church of St Teresa of Lisieux – confirming and strengthening this bond with Lisieux – and St Thérèse (Thérèse, Theresa, Teresa – the variants are interchangeable).

The region was inhabited by a Gallic tribe known as the Lexovii in Gallo-Roman times, the inhabitants still being known as Lexoviens today. It suffered its fair share of continental conflicts with destruction by barbarians in the 5th century, pillaged by the Normans in the 9th, and reduced by siege in the 12th century by Geoffrey Plantaganet, father of Henry II of England. Thomas à Beckett, Henry II's archbishop of Canterbury, took refuge here for a period during his seven years exile from England. It was often the subject of dispute during the tangled conflicts of English and French monarchies during the Hundred-Years War (1337-1453). In medieval times the town was a prestigious centre of local industry and the seat of a powerful bishopric, which was suppressed in 1802 by the Napoleonic Concordat following the French Revolution.

By the turn of the 20th century it contributed significantly to the French textile and leather industries – now long since gone. A significant part of the town was destroyed during the Allied advance following D-Day. Despite the bombardments and fierce fighting through the town, the Cathedral, Carmel, St Thérèse's family home and the almost-completed Basilica were left largely unscathed. The few, remaining half-timbered buildings in and around the town give some flavour of its pre-war days.

Pilgrim destination

Today it is a major pilgrim destination in France, where pilgrims from all over the world come to venerate and seek the intercession of its exalted daughter, Thérèse Martin, the canonised Carmelite nun, St Thérèse of the Child Jesus and the Holy Face.

There is plenty in Lisieux for the pilgrim to absorb – to learn and reflect on what St Thérèse stands for, her impact since her death, and what has been achieved through her intercession. There is certainly a day's worth of gentle 'pilgrimaging' if one is to fully take in the magnificent Basilica dedicated to St Thérèse, the dignified Gothic cathedral of St Peter, the homely cosy environment of the Martin family home – Les Buissonnets, and the intimate and prayerful atmosphere of the Carmel chapel, where Thérèse's mortal remains are placed. Taken all together it will give a perfect picture of her family life, her life in the Carmel, and what has happened since her death and canonisation.

All these places are within easy walking distance within the town. Except for Les Buissonnets, they are all open and accessible all year round, although opening and closing times may vary, depending on the season. Les Buissonnets is closed Christmas and New Year days, and closes annually from mid-November to mid-December. Details of these times can be obtained from the Sanctuary website (listed at the back), the Pilgrim Bureau close to the Carmel, in rue de Carmel, or the Tourist Information Office just opposite the Carmel, at rue d'Alençon.

If you want to extend your pilgrimage there are two very reasonably-priced and well-run pilgrim accommodations associated with the Basilica: Ermitage

Sainte Thérèse, and Foyer Louis et Zélie Martin, again, details from the Sanctuary website.

Lisieux is not overwhelmed by the plethora of shops selling religious artefacts that encircle the Sanctuary at Lourdes; it is very low-key here, only a couple of shops on the approach up to the Basilica.

About this book

The purpose of this book is threefold. Firstly, it is intended as a pilgrim's companion to those who are specifically going to Lisieux on pilgrimage. It will take you to the principal places of Thérèse, provide you with a coherent commentary, which will hopefully obviate the usual copious thumbing, shuffling and cross-referencing through guide and prayer books assorted – either French or English! It also suggests some appropriate prayers and meditations at each place.

Secondly, for those of you on holiday in the region, it may be worth just slipping this in with your travel guides – and if the weather misbehaves – it can, at least, provide a useful alternative activity – a visit to see the Basilica alone is well worth while!

Lastly, it may whet the appetite of those involved in the visit of her Relics to England and Wales in autumn 2009, and indeed, of anyone who happens to bump into her during their life – and lead them to Lisieux to find out more about Thérèse and her times.

While Thérèse's life is well known it is not covered in any detail here, though her story is sketched in the next chapter and snippets will emerge as you follow the pilgrim trail. There are abundant publications, of which those of the CTS make a good start – their small, easily digestible books on her life and spirituality are listed at the back. This is more about the place, and how to appreciate it, thereby hopefully enabling a deeper appreciation of who St Thérèse is, and how she brought herself, and us with her, closer to God. There are also many, many websites dealing with Thérèse, and two current principal ones, which will be sufficient to lead you fully into the subject, are listed in the References at the back.

"I experienced no regret whatsoever at leaving Alençon; children are fond of change, and it was with pleasure that I came to Lisieux."

St Thérèse of Lisieux.

Who is Saint Thérèse?

Much has been written about Saint Thérèse – and of which much is easily and readily available. Thérèse herself wrote, under obedience, much about herself as well – and through her autobiography, *Story of a Soul*, you can gain deep insight into her life and times, and especially her spirituality. Suffice it though, for this small book on Lisieux, for a thumbnail sketch, placing this extraordinary person into some sort of context with this very ordinary place; the place where Thérèse lived most of her childhood, before disappearing into the enclosure of the Lisieux Carmel for the rest of her life.

So, who was Marie-Françoise-Thérèse Martin, to give her full baptismal name, later to become Sister Thérèse of the Child Jesus and the Holy Face, to give her full, professed name? Why does she continue to have such an impact on the Church and people's lives, to this day, all round the world? On the face of it, she was no-one special: just one of the many hundreds of anonymous Carmelite nuns faithfully living out her vocation of work, prayer and love in her convent in Normandy in the late 19th century.

Family life

Thérèse was born in 1873 in the French town of Alençon, the youngest child of a family of nine. Her father, Louis, was a watchmaker, and her mother, Zélie, a lace maker. It was a pious (in the best sense!), loving and devoted family, which Thérèse was to look back on: "The good Lord was pleased to surround me with love. My first memories are imprinted with the most tender smiles and caresses." As recognition of their faith and love of God, their family, and of each other, Louis and Zélie Martin were beatified by Pope Benedict XVI in October 2008 – the only married couple, to my knowledge, earning this unique tribute within the context of marriage and family life.

Family life was not easy though. Four children – two boys and two girls – died in early childhood. Further tragedy struck the family when Zélie suffered a painful and untimely death from breast cancer when Thérèse was only four years old. This premature death provoked a family move to the nearby town of Lisieux, where Thérèse's father could be close to his sister-in-law's family for support.

The death of her mother had a profound effect on Thérèse's early childhood, gradually withdrawing into herself, until at one stage, when she was ten, she sickened to the point of family and friends fearing for her life. It was only when praying with her sisters on her sickbed, that through the powerful and telling intercession of Our Lady, she was healed.

Vocational calling

That she had a deep spiritual inclination, even as a child, was obvious, "As I grew up, I loved God more and more, and I frequently made Him the offering of my heart, using the words my mother had taught me. I strove to please Jesus in all my actions and I guarded with great care against ever offending Him."

Thérèse's calling to the religious life was something she felt very strongly too, very early on. In her determination to enter Carmel as soon as she possibly could, this shy, reserved girl sought, and was granted, a personal interview with her Bishop, but to no avail. When in Rome with her father, attending a pilgrim audience with Pope Leo XIII, and despite being told by an official that no-one should speak directly to the Pope, she calmly went up and knelt in front of him to petition her cause. His reply, although not a direct 'yes' was, "If you enter, it will be God's will."

However, she continued to draw strength from the unstinting support of her father, and with continuing interviews with senior clergy, she at last achieved her goal, entering the Carmelite convent at Lisieux at the tender age of fifteen, proclaiming, "At last the doors of the Carmel closed behind me, and there I received the embraces of the two beloved sisters [her sisters Pauline and Marie] who had each been a mother to me, and of a new family whose loving devotedness is unknown to the world."

Convent life

As she settled to convent life she found that her tender years and her ardour were not going to curry any favours, particularly from the Prioress and the Novice Mistress. But to Thérèse, these personal rebuffs were part of the many lessons that she was learning on the way to attaining the pure, selfless and detached love – freed from the chains of subjective human affections – that shines out from her spiritual approach. But whatever her community made of her, it was clear to them that here was someone who, although so young in years, was developing and quietly displaying a profound depth of wisdom, humility and spirituality.

At the time of her entry to Carmel, her beloved father started experiencing bouts of paralysis, at times not recognising his daughters. He was eventually taken into a nursing home and died six years after Thérèse had entered Carmel. "Words cannot express my agony. I shall not try to describe it."

In September 1890 she made her Profession, and in 1893 she was appointed to help with the novitiates' instruction, choosing to live within the novitiate, despite being entitled to live in the slightly more salubrious surroundings of the professed nuns. It was here, during her periods of instruction and her conversations at recreation periods, that the Prioress was persuaded of the value of her utterings, and directed Thérèse to start writing about her childhood experiences and her thoughts, which she did, with some trepidation, during her leisure moments.

Suffering

In early 1896, having struggled through a virulent influenza epidemic which swept through the convent, indications of serious illness began to manifest. She had contracted tuberculosis which spread to her intestines, leading to a period of prolonged and painful suffering. During this period she also suffered a darkness of the soul, experiencing continual temptations and doubts over her faith. In her typical manner she managed to turn her sufferings to practical effect. A sister, querying her painful progress as she took her short daily walk, received the response, "I offer each step for a missionary. I recollect that in a distant land one of them is perhaps worn out by his labours. To lessen this fatigue I offer mine to God." All the while, she continued with her writings.

After only nine years in Carmel, aged twenty four, and after months of prolonged suffering, Thérèse humbly surrendered her mortal life, her eyes fixed on the object of her love – the Crucified Christ – as she murmured her last words, "Oh! I love Him... my God... I love you!"

Spirituality and miracles

It was only when her profound spiritual writings –
Histoire d'une Âme (*The Story of a Soul*) – gradually
emerged to the world that the significance of her ministry,
and the depth of her spirituality, began to be realised. At
the heart of her writings is her discovery of her vocation
of Love, and applying it through her life and her prayer:
"...in the heart of the Church...I shall be Love." At the
heart of her life was her expression of her Little Way of
Spiritual Childhood, and how she actually lived and
professed it, striving for simple perfection and for
perfection in simplicity. She developed a trusting,
childlike reliance on God's love, a joyful realisation that
'littleness' was the way to approach God. She also
realised that holiness was not necessarily accomplished
by great heroic acts, or 'great deeds', but could be built
upon by achieving the small things, the boring things, the
irritating things, with care – through "doing of the least of
things for love."

She had a great love of the Scriptures, resorting with
relief to the Bible after learned treatises on spirituality
had left "my head splitting and my heart parched," and
when doing so, "...all seems luminous, a single word
opens up infinite horizons to my soul, perfection seems
easy; I see that it is enough to realise one's nothingness,
and give oneself wholly, like a child, into the arms of the

good God. Leaving to great souls, great minds, the fine books I cannot understand, I rejoice to be little because 'only children, and those who are like them, will be admitted to the heavenly banquet'."

With the spread of *Histoire* came the manifestation of countless miracles and conversions associated with her intercession – many accompanied by the sweet smelling scent of roses. From these, a world wide devotion rapidly spread, transcending place, age, gender, status or beliefs. The response to this growing evidence from the Popes of the time was to hasten the whole process of canonisation, backed, in Pius XI's words, "by the supplication of the whole Catholic world."

Sainthood

She was canonised in May 1925 by Pope Pius XI, who declared her 'the beloved star of my pontificate'; in December 1927 she was proclaimed by Pius as Patroness of Missions. On Missionary Sunday in October 1997, a hundred years after her death, she was declared a Doctor of the Church by Pope John Paul II – the youngest, and third woman. In his proclamation homily he noted that despite being, "the youngest of all the Doctors of the Church, her ardent spiritual journey shows such maturity and the insights of faith expressed in her writings are so vast and profound that they deserve a place among the great spiritual masters." She is the Patron Saint of missions and missionaries, AIDS sufferers, aviators, the sick, florists, loss of parents, outreach to Russia, and tuberculosis sufferers, to name some! Her Feast Day throughout the Universal Church is celebrated on 1st October.

You will always recognise statues of St Thérèse – dressed in her cream cloak and brown Carmelite habit, or, if in monochrome, she will always be seen holding to her breast a Crucifix and a bunch of roses. The Crucifix identifies her with the Lord's suffering on the Cross, and through that her ardent desire – and prayers – for the salvation of souls. The roses symbolise her stated promise that, "I want to spend my heaven doing good upon earth... I shall let fall a shower of roses."

These showers of roses have been made manifest by the many conversions achieved through her example and writings, and through the many visible and unseen physical and spiritual miracles achieved through her intercession. One of her ardent desires was to be a missionary bringing the Gospel message to the world – something clearly unachievable from the confines of an enclosed convent – but something she has clearly achieved – through God's grace – by the visit of her relics to over forty countries of the world, and the graces that have flowed from that.

She particularly appeals to young people as a role model; but the poor, the sick, priests and missionaries, families in trouble, prisoners, those whose faith is on the wane, as well as those with no particular concern – all have been touched – and those in need have been immeasurably comforted, strengthened and healed by her intercession. Her appeal is universal – and will continue to endure until the end of time.

"Love proves itself by deeds, so how am I to show my love? Great deeds are forbidden me. The only way I can prove my love is by scattering flowers, and these flowers are every little sacrifice, every glance and word, and the doing of the least actions for love."

The Basilica of St Thérèse.

Tribute to St Thérèse – The Basilica

Construction

Soon after the canonisation of St Thérèse in 1925, Lisieux rapidly grew as a centre of pilgrimage. It was obvious that the small Carmel chapel and surrounds was not going to be sufficient for the swiftly growing numbers of pilgrims. Although there was some opposition from local clergy – on the grounds that Lisieux already had plenty of churches and that devotion to Thérèse, mainly by French soldiers of the First World War, may have had its day – plans, instigated by the Bishop of the day, went ahead to design a new fitting sanctuary to honour the newly canonised saint. Support for the project gathered momentum when Pope Pius XI, who considered Thérèse as the 'star of his pontificate', gave strong endorsement to the idea. With the active participation of Thérèse's sisters in the design process – Mother Agnes, Prioress of the Carmel, and Sister Geneviève – work got under way. The foundation stone was laid and blessed by the Papal Nuncio in 1929. An international Eucharistic Congress was held in the largely completed Basilica in July 1937, at which it was blessed by Cardinal Pacelli, the future Pope Pius XII.

The onset of the Second World War slowed progress, and construction work was modest – the main feature being the building of the cloister wings. Although about 120 bombs fell in and around the Basilica in the initial D-Day bombing raids on Lisieux in August 1944, it was left largely undamaged – testament to the robust construction. The Basilica crypt also sheltered the Sisters from the Carmel, St Thérèse's relics, and many civilians and refugees during the bombing and subsequent fighting. Further and possibly total damage by the advancing Allied forces on what would have been a significant military target – given its dominating position over the town – is attributed to Major George Warren of the 1/6 Battalion Queen's Royal Regiment. He made a point of specifically briefing the commander of the advancing armoured assault on Lisieux that the Basilica did not hold any German defences, thus sparing it.

Completion and Consecration

After the war, the effort went into completing the interior mosaics. Although the bulk of major construction was completed and paid for within ten years of commencement, it was not until 1954 that the completed Basilica was finally consecrated by the Archbishop of Rouen, in the presence of the Archbishop of Paris, representing the Pope. Even so, it was a remarkably short construction and completion period, given the size and complexity, and given the fact that cathedral constructions are usually measured in half centuries or more! Pope Pius XI's wish that it be 'very big, very beautiful and built very quickly' was certainly fulfilled.

This massive structure, with a footprint of 4,500 square metres and 90 metres tall, is one of the largest churches built in the 20th century – in silhouette it matches Notre-Dame in Paris and St Patrick's Cathedral, New York. It is built in the neo-Byzantine style, using a particularly high quality, durable stone, from a specially selected quarry 100 kilometres away, and from the stonework on a sunny day, you can see the glinting of flecks of quartz and mica. Inside, the mosaics cover a staggering 8,000 square metres. There was no State or Church funding – finance was raised by public subscription; through many thousands of small donations – the 'pennies of the poor' - from every age and walk of life; from France and worldwide. For instance, a young girl wrote in enclosing five francs, explaining that she willingly gave up her lemonade that week *pour Thérèse*.

The Approach

As soon as you turn into the Avenue of St Thérèse to head up to the Basilica from the town below, you will immediately be struck by its impressive, imposing form – the vast dome and substructure filling the skyline. As you enter the Basilica grounds you will see a large statue of

22

St Thérèse welcomes visitors with the 'New Message'.

Thérèse, her right hand held high, proclaiming what she holds in her left hand – the open Scriptures, on which are inscribed two words: *Omen Novum*: the New Sign, or New Message that Thérèse brings to all who approach her. The Basilica is set in extensive, pine-wooded grounds on a hilltop overlooking the town. On reaching the spacious, neat, gravelled parvis in front of the church it may be worth just pausing a moment to take it all in and get your bearings, for there are many aspects to look at.

In front of you, the loom of this magnificent building, with its slender flanking towers, and wide stairway inviting you up to the deep, arched entrance set in the great, gleaming, solid façade. Striking boldly out from each side of the façade are two raised, galleried cloisters, each ending with a chunky but intricately fashioned tower, crowned with distinct coned domes. As you will discover later during your visit, underneath the left-hand cloister, at ground level, there is a charming diorama displaying aspects of Thérèse's life. Beneath the right-hand cloister, there is the cinema where viewings of a short documentary on Thérèse's life are shown during the high season (for viewings in English, enquire at the Information desk in the Pastoral Centre). Entrance to the Crypt and Blessed Sacrament chapel is also made from here. All in all, this solid structure is a bold statement of strength and permanence, radiating St Thérèse's characteristics of determination and enduring mission.

To the right, and away from the main Basilica, is the unusual, free-standing obelisk-shaped campanile, or bell tower. Opposite the church, at the other side of the terrace, but sunk discretely lower in the hillside, the newly-built Pastoral Reception Centre. Out of immediate sight, round the back of the Basilica, there are Stations of the Cross cut into the hillside, and the former tomb of Thérèse's parents, Blessed Louis and Zélie Martin.

On this occasion, I broke my usual practice of wandering round the outside to build up anticipation before entering, because I knew I would be distracted by other features in the grounds. I headed instead, down to the spacious, modern, well organised Pastoral Centre to try and gather some sense and feeling for the whole before going into the Basilica. Here, there is a well-stocked shop and other information and displays about all aspects of the Basilica and St Thérèse.

INSIDE

Before entering the Basilica, St Thérèse greets you from high on the front façade, in the centre of the top pediment. She is surrounded by angels, and, at the lower level, by all those on earth who contributed to her glorification. In the columned gallery just below, there is a depiction of the virtues of Faith, Hope, Charity, Justice, Prudence, Fortitude and Temperance. Above the doors, the tympanum, showing Jesus with a child at His

Inside the Basilica - "... space - mosaics - arches..."

knees, explaining to the Apostles gathered round Him, "…anyone who does not welcome the kingdom of God like a little child, will never enter it" (*Mk* 10:15).

On entering, first impressions that may hit you quite forcibly: space, mosaics, arches, probably in that order! The size of the interior is staggering. The wide, single nave, the height, and then the dome reaching up above that, all amplify this. There are uninterrupted views of the sanctuary from all parts of the church – no pillars to obstruct. A shallow transept crosses the church half way down, topped by the soaring cupola. Huge, strong arches support the church from rear to front, leading down, in a series of stepped arches, to the final more delicate arch surrounding the apse, all producing a rather unusual but satisfying symmetry.

Mosaics

The mosaics – in a bold, contemporary and explicit style – cover just about every inch of wall and ceiling surface. The series designed to draw your eye immediately, are those round the expansive arched area above the sanctuary and apse. At the top of the arch – God the Father, arms outstretched, sending down the Holy Spirit.

In the apse, below, the central mosaic of Jesus, arms open wide in acceptance, His protecting cloak being held open by Our Lady and St Thérèse, with the lambs seeking shelter under it. Around the apse are the words: 'Come to me all you who labour and are burdened'. There are many other mosaic themes to examine as you go round, all reflecting the Scriptures and aspects of Thérèse's life. For instance, Thérèse loved angels, and this is reflected explicitly by the prominent angel mosaics on the dome supports, and indeed many other angels throughout the Basilica and crypt.

As you start to wander around, certain other features emerge. Around the side walls are eighteen uniformly-arched, shallow side chapels, each one donated by a country, which you can examine in detail.

Reliquary

As you move on down the right-hand side, you will see, in the right transept above the blaze of massed devotional candles, the reliquary of St Thérèse. The elaborate, gilded and glass fronted casket, donated by Pope Pius XI, displays a bone from St Thérèse's right arm. It is here that devotion is centred, with the faithful kneeling, praying, meditating – focussing on the tangible, physical presence of her mortal remains – and through that focus, seeking her divine intercession and inspiration.

Prayer

Miraculous Invocation to St Thérèse of the Child Jesus
O Glorious St Thérèse, whom Almighty God has raised up to aid and inspire the human family, I implore your Miraculous Intercession. You are so powerful in obtaining

every need of body and spirit from the Heart of God. Holy Mother Church proclaims you "Prodigy of Miracles... the Greatest Saint of Modern Times." Now I fervently beseech you to answer my petition (mention here) *and to carry out your promises of spending Heaven doing good upon earth, of letting fall from Heaven a Shower of Roses. Little Flower, give me your childlike faith, to see the Face of God in the people and experiences of my life, and to love God with full confidence. St Thérèse, my Carmelite Sister, I will fulfil your plea "to be made known everywhere" and I will continue to lead others to Jesus through you. Amen.*

The Dome

Moving into the centre of the transept and craning your neck to examine the dome mosaic, you will see, in the golden blaze of the cupola, Thérèse accepting her crown of sainthood from Jesus and Our Lady, with the anointing hand of the Father, above them. You will also note the deep barrel of the dome pierced by delicate, arched stained-glass windows at the top; then, mosaics of the eight Beatitudes themed with the Saints of the Church. Under the mosaics, the delicately arched viewing gallery, where one can examine these mosaics more closely, and peer down into the Basilica. From the exterior gallery there are commanding views of the town and surrounding country side (the gallery is open only in the high season).

At the base of the barrel, Thérèse's well known promise: "I want to spend my Heaven doing good upon earth...I shall let fall a shower of roses."

Whilst still in the centre of the transept, look up left to the north transept at the so-called 'blue stained-glass window' depicting the Good Shepherd; and then to the right (south) transept, to the 'red stained-glass window', showing Thérèse's deep desire to receive Jesus' love through His suffering on the Cross. Before moving back away from the transept area, note the side chapel, third one back on the left-hand side, donated by England. It is dedicated to St George and St Thomas à Beckett. There are also chapels given by Scotland and Ireland.

When you finally turn to go to the rear exit, you will see the large mosaic above the doors, showing Thérèse surrounded by all those personalities who furthered her cause, with, to the left and right, the nations of the world looking on.

Statue

Finally, as you reach the rear of the church, by the corner side chapel donated by Poland, the iconic statue of Thérèse embracing a Crucifix and roses, brightly illuminated, and surrounded by a profusion of votive offerings: plaques, medals, flowers, cards and written prayer requests. One note that caught my eye, in the wobbly handwriting of a child – in English – was the earnest request, "Please keep my family safe and my friends", accompanied by the childlike, spidery drawings of said family and friends. Such is the appeal and the trust evoked by St Thérèse, even to little children.

As you reflect by this statue, you may wish to consider what Thérèse said about prayer:

"For me prayer is an aspiration of the heart, it is a simple glance directed to heaven, it is a cry of gratitude and love in the midst of trial, as well as joy; finally, it is something great, supernatural, which expands my soul and unites me to Jesus."

THE CRYPT

In many cathedrals and churches the crypt is often the poor relation – dusty, neglected, underutilised and forlorn. But here, this crypt is the jewel of the Basilica. Immediately on entry, you will be struck by the contrast. The extensive mosaics are more delicate and subtle in their pastel colours and in their finely detailed composition. With its three be-pillared and arched naves, it is spacious, airy and light, giving off a sense of joy and vitality, as well as intimacy. And in encapsulating this I want to take you straight to the statue of St Thérèse at the front, in the apse – her arms held high and wide, her joyful face looking upwards, and which, combined with the mosaic behind, looks as

The Basilica Crypt.

though she is throwing a cascade of roses heavenward. She is flanked by many angels, offering her baskets full of roses, all overarched by a gleaming rainbow and her final words summing up her sole desire: "Oh! I love Him...my God...I love you!"

Thérèse's spirituality

"Whoever is a little one let him come to me" (Pr 9:4)

The whole crypt is themed throughout with a profusion of wild flowers and birds, reflecting Thérèse's love of nature and Creation. But overall the theme reflects Thérèse's spirituality. This is evident by the portrayal of the Beatitudes on the eight pillars of the nave, and in the choice of the six side chapels round the crypt, dedicated to her twelve favourite Saints: St Mary Magdalene, St Cecilia, St Teresa d'Avila, St Francis de Sales, St Paul, St Joseph, St John of the Cross, St Joan of Arc, St John the Evangelist, Bl Théophane Vénard (French missionary, martyred in IndoChina in 1861), St Agnes and St Augustine. Other mosaics portray key events in Thérèse's life: Baptism, first Holy Communion, her miraculous cure, receiving the Carmelite habit, and her death.

Meditation

Here is the perfect meditation, written by St Thérèse, for your surroundings in the crypt:

Jesus deigned to teach me this mystery. He set before me the book of nature; I understand how all the flowers He has created are beautiful, how the splendour of the rose and the whiteness of the lily do not take away the perfume of the little violet or the delightful simplicity of the daisy. I understand that if all flowers wanted to be roses, nature would lose her springtime beauty, and the fields would no longer be decked out with little wild flowers.

And so it is in the world of souls, Jesus' garden. He willed to create great souls comparable to lilies and roses, but He has created smaller ones and these must be content to be daisies or violets destined to give joy to God's glances when He looks down at his feet. Perfection consists in doing His will, in being what He wills us to be.

Blessed Louis and Zélie Martin

The right hand side-chapel, dedicated to Our Lady, has a copy of the statue of *la Vierge du Sourire* – the Virgin of the Smile – the channel of grace instrumental in Thérèse's cure from serious illness as a child. The original statue, taken from her home, Les Buissonnets, is above her reliquary in the Carmel chapel, down in the town.

The left-hand side-chapel – dedicated to the Child Jesus, again with a replica of a statue associated with Thérèse which is seen next to her in a group photograph of the Carmelite Sisters – is of particular interest. There you will be able to venerate the

prominently displayed reliquary of Thérèse's parents –
Louis and Zélie Martin – placed here since their
Beatification on 19th October 2008. The reliquary
casket is a gift from the people of Ireland.

Prayer for intercession of Blessed Louis and Zélie Martin

God of eternal love,
You give us Blessed Louis and Zélie Martin,
the parents of St Thérèse, as an example of holiness
  in marriage.
They remained faithful to You and your commandments
in all the duties and trials of life.
They desired to raise their children to become saints.
May their prayers and example
help Christian family life to blossom in our world today.
If it be your will, grant us the grace we now ask of You...,
through the intercession of Blessed
  Louis and Zélie Martin,
and let them be counted among the Saints
  in your Church.
Through Jesus Christ our Lord. Amen.

Blessed Sacrament Chapel

Directly off to the left of the crypt is the recently
constructed Blessed Sacrament chapel (2000) – a quiet
place for recollection and prayer. It is plain, simple and

unadorned. Muted daylight filters in from shrouded skylights above. Over the tabernacle is a large copy of Roublev's icon – the Three Persons of the Holy Trinity at the communion table, with that invitation for you to fill the fourth, vacant place and complete the circle round the table.

Meditation in front of the Blessed Sacrament

I need a heart burning with tenderness,
Who will be my support for ever,
Who loves everything in me, even my weakness,
And who never leaves me day or night.
I could find no creature
Who could always love me day or night.
I could find no creature
Who could always love me and never die.
I must have a God who takes on my nature
And becomes my brother and is able to suffer!
You heard me, only Friend whom I love.
To ravish my heart, You became man.
You shed Your blood, what a supreme mystery!

O Heart of Jesus, treasure of tenderness,
You Yourself are my happiness, my only hope.
You who knew how to charm my tender youth,
Stay near me till the last night.

Ah! I know well, all our righteousness
Is worthless in Your sight.

To give value to my sacrifices,
I want to cast them into Your Divine Heart.
You did not find Your angels without blemish.
In the midst of lightning You gave Your law!
I hide myself in Your Sacred Heart, Jesus.
I do not fear, my virtue is You! (St Thérèse of Lisieux)

As you exit the crypt you will see over the rear two arches a particularly powerful and beautiful mosaic of the Holy Trinity – the Father holding up the Cross from behind, with the Crucified Son gazing up at both Father and Holy Spirit. Arching over the Trinity, held aloft by two flanking angels, are the words *Dieu est Charité* – 'God is Love'.

OUTSIDE

At some stage it would be worth taking a slow walk round the exterior of this magnificent church. In doing this, and looking up as you go round, will you soon recognise and appreciate the sheer bulk and ambitions of this solid building, with its many intricacies of design and construction. At the back you can take in the large carved, bas-relief Stations of the Cross, grouped together three Stations at a time, culminating in an altar above, overlooking Calvary. Beneath each Station, carved in French, English and Spanish are some of the well-known quotes of St Thérèse. Below the Stations is the former tomb of Louis and Zélie Martin – their remains disinterred and translated to the crypt on their Beatification.

You may also hear the beautiful ringing tunes of many of the 51 bells in the campanile – playing intricate, delicate, sonorous music, a special treat to hear. The heaviest bell in the campanile, hung in 1948, weighs in at some 10 tonnes, and is named 'Thérèse Protectress of the peoples'. The full carillon was completed in Jubilee Year, 2000, with the hanging of the last two bells, of which the heaviest weighing in at a mere 1050 kgs was named 'St Thérèse of the Child Jesus and Holy Face – Doctor of the Church'.

It is also worth touring the diorama under the left hand cloister – twelve tasteful, sweet waxwork scenes of aspects of Thérèse's life, accompanied by an audio commentary. In the low season, viewing of the documentary film of Thérèse is done by appointment with the desk in the Pastoral Centre and watched in a viewing room in the Centre.

"At the beginning of my spiritual life when I was thirteen or fourteen, I used to ask myself what I would have to strive for later on because I believed it was quite impossible for me to understand perfection better. I learned very quickly since then that the more one advances, the more one sees the goal is still far off. And now I am simply resigned to see myself always imperfect and in this I find my joy."

Inside the Cathedral of St Peter.

The Family's Place of Prayer
- Cathedral of St Peter

During my time in Lisieux I grew to love this dignified, careworn building – inevitably overshadowed by the splendid, modern Basilica up on the hill, but to where I was continually drawn. St Peter's cathedral can not even claim its own bishop, the See having been suppressed in 1802 by the Napoleonic Concordat after the French Revolution, and it is now part of the diocese of Bayeux (Lisieux). But this was the Martin family's church – Thérèse's church – around which their daily Catholic life revolved, and it probably has not changed much since her day, lending it a poignant authenticity.

Town centre cathedral

The cathedral is set near the centre of town, and rather hemmed in on three sides by surrounding buildings. On the fourth side there is a delightful, well tended public park – *Jardin de l'évêché* (garden of the bishop's palace) overlooked by what was the Bishop's Palace – ideal for a rest or a picnic when visiting the town. The cathedral, built in the Gothic style, was started at the end of the 12th century, and completed in the 13th and 16th centuries. It portrays dignified, graceful beauty, which shines through the centuries of wear and tear. It was one of the few buildings in Lisieux to survive intact the allied invasion of the Second World War.

The main entrance into the west façade is off a small public square, below the two mismatched towers, one with a steeple, and the other with a blunt, tiled roof. Inside there are no displays of stunning stained glass windows, no profusion of statuary or carving, such as Chartres – it is plain, unadorned, and simple – modestly displaying its exquisite architecture. It has three long, be-pillared and arched naves with numerous side chapels and a shallow transept, off which from the south is the other main entrance from the street. The plain, flagged floor, worn smooth over the centuries emphasises the simplicity and durability, and the battered pillar bases give testament to its age and use over the years.

Traces of Thérèse

As you start to wander round from back left, you can trace visible evidence of Thérèse's, and the Martin family's, involvement here. You come across a bronze statue of St Peter, a replica of that in St Peter's, Rome, the right foot worn to a shine from the touch of passing pilgrims, no doubt passed many times by Thérèse in the same manner.

In the first side chapel on the left, the confessional where Thérèse made her confessions. On recalling her first confession here she writes, "Oh! Dear Mother, with what care you prepared me for my first confession, telling me it was not a man but to God I was about to tell my sins: I was very much convinced of this truth. I made my confession in a great spirit of faith, even asking you if I had to tell Father Ducellier I love him with all my heart as it was to God in person I was speaking."

As testament to his faith and thanksgiving, Louis Martin donated the intricately carved, white marble high altar as a votive offering in 1888, not long before he was admitted, in February 1889, to a psychiatric hospital in Caen. In Thérèse's mind both were very much linked, commenting, "Papa has just offered God an altar; but it was he who was the victim chosen to be sacrificed on it along with the unblemished lamb."

Chapels

At the top end of the ambulatory, the slender Lady chapel in which the Blessed Sacrament is reserved, built in the 15th century by the then bishop, Pierre Cauchon, a judge at Joan of Arc's trial. Here, Thérèse attended Mass during the week, and was also where she prayed for the repentance of the notorious murderer facing execution, Pranzini, in 1887, her first 'child' in her quest for the salvation of souls.

Meditation

St John of the Cross (1591) – the 'Mystical Doctor' and Carmelite, whose writing was piercing and uncompromising – was very much one of Thérèse's spiritual role models:

A genuine spirit seeks the distasteful in God rather than the delectable, leans more towards suffering than towards consolation, more toward going without everything for God rather than toward possession. It prefers dryness and affliction to sweet consolation. It knows that this is the significance of following Christ and denying self, that the other method is perhaps a seeking of self in God – something entirely contrary to love. Seeking oneself in God is the same as looking for the caresses and consolations of God. Seeking God in oneself entails not only the desire of doing without these consolations for God's sake, but also the inclination to choose for love in Christ all that is most distasteful whether in God or in the world – and such is the love of God. (St John of the Cross)

Thérèse echoes this: "*Living on Love is not setting up one's tent at the top of Tabor. It is climbing Calvary with Jesus, it is looking at the Cross as a treasure…*"

The side chapel in the right hand corner of the ambulatory was rented by the Martin family for Sunday

Mass. A modern statue of Thérèse praying in front of the Crucifix evokes the moment when, aged fourteen, she felt the overwhelming desire to become a missionary. One Sunday in Mass a picture of the Crucified Christ partly protruded from her Missal, showing only one hand of Jesus. On seeing it she experienced, "a new and expressible feeling... I was struck by the blood flowing from one of the divine hands. I felt a great pang of sorrow when thinking this blood was falling to the ground without anyone's hastening to gather it up. I was resolved to remain in spirit at the foot of the Cross and to gather up this divine dew. I understood I was then to pour it out on souls."

Meditation

This meditation, very apt at this point, was composed by St Teresa of Avila (d. 1582), namesake, fellow Carmelite, fellow Doctor of the Church, and one of Thérèse's spiritual heroines and mentors. These words would have struck powerfully with her – and maybe they did – possibly pulling her in two directions: one, the yearning for the salvation of souls through 'diligence and prayer', as with Pranzini, and secondly, her great desire, in her words, to, "travel over the whole earth to preach Your Name and to plant Your glorious Cross on infidel soil." In her lifetime in Carmel, she achieved the former; in her death and afterlife, with her writings going worldwide,

Thérèse kneeling at the family side chapel.

and her relics having been taken to over forty countries of the world, she has achieved the latter:

A Franciscan friar happened to come and see me... a great servant of God, who had the same desire for the good of souls as I, but he was able to transfer them into deeds for which I envied him greatly. He had recently come back from the Indies. He began to tell me about the many millions of souls that were being lost there for want of Christian instruction, and before leaving he gave us a sermon or conference, encouraging us to do penance. I was so grief-stricken over the loss of so many souls that I couldn't contain myself. I went to a hermitage with many tears. I cried out to the Lord, begging him that he give me the means to be able to do something to win some souls to his service, since the devil was carrying away so many, and that my prayer would do some good since I wasn't able to do anything else. I was very envious of those who for love of Our Lord were able to be engaged in winning souls, though they might suffer a thousand deaths. And thus it happens to me that when we read in the lives of the saints that they converted souls, I feel much greater devotion, tenderness, and envy than over all the martyrdoms they suffered. This is the inclination the Lord has given me, for it seems to me that he prizes a soul that through our diligence and prayer we gain for him, through his mercy, more than all the services we can render him. (St Teresa of Avila)

Continuing your tour back on down, you will come to a statue of Our Lady of Carmel in the first side chapel past the transept, in front of which her sister, Pauline, used to pray. Lastly, in one of the central side chapels, a picture of the Holy Face, an image in which Thérèse would spend much time in contemplating, and from which she took part of her professed name, proclaiming, "Ah! I desired that, like the face of Jesus, 'my face be truly hidden, that no one on earth would know me' (*Is* 53:3). I thirsted after suffering and I longed to be forgotten."

"One can never have too much confidence in the good God. I shall love him to the point of recklessness. I will never put limits to my confidence."

Thérèse's Family Home - Les Buissonnets

In a quiet, inner suburb of Lisieux, a few short minutes' walk from the cathedral, is the Martin family house – Les Buissonnets (The Thicket, or Bushes) – to where the family moved after her mother's death, and where Thérèse spent eleven years in 'this beautiful cradle of my childhood'. The house was on a small side-road next to a park called Jardin de l'Étoile – Garden of the Star. In Thérèse's words on first sighting, "The house appeared very charming to me: a belvedere from which a view extended far into the distance, an English garden in front, and a large vegetable garden in the rear of the house, all this was a new joy to my young imagination. In fact, this smiling habitation became the theatre of many sweet joys and unforgettable family scenes. Elsewhere, as I said above, I was an exile, I wept, I felt I no longer had a mother! There, my heart expanded and I smiled once more at life."

And on first approaching, looking up at its slightly elevated position – yes, it is a charming house: late 18th-century, built of warm, red brick, with attractive pale stone mullions framing the numerous windows – there is one large central four-windowed gable (Thérèse's

Les Buissonnets - The Martin family home.

'belvedere'), behind which was Louis' office, flanked by two single-window gables, all set in the roof. It sits within relatively small, but attractive gardens, front and rear. Previously it may have been two properties, as there are two mirroring doors on the front façade.

Inside

The feature that immediately took me quite by surprise was the front door entering directly into the small kitchen. It is dominated by a large, homely red brick and timber-surround fireplace, where the family's meals were cooked over the wood fire. The red and white, smooth tiled floor and half wood panelling, adds to the warm, cosy look. The kitchen holds great significance for Thérèse, for it was here on return from midnight Mass on Christmas Eve 1886, aged thirteen, that she "received the grace of leaving my childhood, in a word, the grace of my complete conversion."

It came about by overhearing a remark made by her father about it being 'the last year' that her shoes would be put by the fireplace to receive her Christmas gifts – the equivalent of 'high time she grew up!' She successfully fought back her childish tears and sensitivities – which had predominated since her mother's death – and confronted the reality of what needed to happen next in her life. "On that night of light began the third period of my life, the most beautiful and the most filled with graces from heaven. The work I had been unable to do in ten years was done by Jesus in one instant, contenting himself with my good will which was never lacking."

There are short audio commentaries given over loudspeakers as you move around the house (make it known that you are English!), and the pace of your tour will be geared to these. Having paused in the kitchen, you will then be invited to look through a display window into the dining room, next door. It is as it was when the family lived there, wood panelled, formal, an ornate dresser and glass fronted cabinet full of glass and crockery, and a surprisingly small round table in the centre. Above the fireplace is a clock made by Louis Martin, the clock maker. Thérèse had her last meal here before entering the Carmel in April, 1888, and in remembering it she remarks, "Ah! How heart rending these family reunions can really be! When you would like to see yourself forgotten, the most tender caresses and words are showered upon you, making the sacrifice of separation felt all the more."

Upstairs

You then move on upstairs into the large bedroom of Thérèse's older sisters, Marie and Pauline. It was here that Thérèse, aged ten, when very seriously ill, was put to be nursed. Family, friends and doctors were at their wits' end over the persistent symptoms, and the prognosis was not good. As she was being prayed over by her sisters Marie, Léonie and Céline, and Thérèse was beseeching Our Lady to take pity. "All of a sudden the Blessed Virgin [in the form of the 'statue of the smile', by her bedside] appeared beautiful to me, so beautiful that never had I seen anything so attractive; her face was suffused with an ineffable benevolence and tenderness, but what penetrated to the very depths of my soul was the 'ravishing smile of the Blessed Virgin'. At that instant all my pain disappeared, and two large tears glistened on my eyelashes, and flowed down my cheeks silently, but they were tears of unmixed joy."

What you see in this room is the outline of the scene of that occasion: the rather solid wooden bed in which Thérèse lay, overlooked by a copy of Our Lady's statue of the smile. Here you may be offered a few moments to quietly reflect. These sweet words about Our Lady, written by Thérèse, are suggested:

Meditation

We know very well that the Blessed Virgin is Queen of heaven and earth, but she is more Mother than Queen; and we should not say, on account of her prerogatives, that she surpasses all the saints in glory just as the sun at its rising makes the stars disappear from sight. My God! How strange that would be! A mother who makes her children's

*glory vanish! I myself think just the contrary. I believe
she'll increase the splendour of the elect very much.*

*It's good to speak about her prerogatives, but we
should not stop at this, and if, in a sermon, we are
obliged from beginning to end to exclaim and say: 'Ah!
Ah! We would grow tired!' who knows whether some soul
would not reach the point of feeling a certain
estrangement from a creature so superior and would not
say: 'If things are such, it's better to go and shine as well
as one is able in some little corner!'*

*What the Blessed Virgin has more than we have is the
privilege of not being able to sin, she was exempt from the
stain of original sin; but on the other hand she wasn't as
fortunate as we are, since she didn't have a Blessed
Virgin to love. And this is one more sweetness for us and
one less sweetness for her!* (St Thérèse of Lisieux)

Now moving on through this top floor you can peer
into Louis Martin's bedroom, noting the elaborate,
canopied wooden bed. But what made a big impression
here was a most beautiful picture – which you view
through the reflected image of a mirror – painted by
sister Céline, showing the Virgin Mary comforting
Mary Magdalene. Sadly, I don't believe there are any
copies available.

The last stop indoors is the bedroom at the back, that
of Léonie – overlooking the rear garden. Here are

displayed many of Thérèse's childhood toys, dolls, clothes and knick knacks. It is a fascinating snapshot of a middle class childhood from a God-fearing family of that era. Taking pride of place in the centre is Thérèse's elaborate First Holy Communion dress with adornments and rosary. The item that particularly caught my eye was the most exquisite dolls' tea set, beautifully retained and displayed in its red velvet case. There is a small repository in this room where you can purchase Thérèse memorabilia.

The garden

On a nice day, you will no doubt finish your visit by going out to the rear garden. It too is a homely place, redbrick and tile-roofed sheds at the back (and toilets!), but you will notice, close to the house a charming statue of Thérèse, sitting by her father, hands clasped together, gazing imploringly into his face. This was the moment when she decided to press her case with him to enter Carmel. "Through my tears I confided my desire to enter Carmel and soon his tears mingled with mine…. He was soon convinced my desire was God's will, and in his deep faith he cried out that God was giving him a great honour in asking his children from him."

Garden Meditation

By St Teresa Benedicta of the Cross (Edith Stein), convert from Judaism, Carmelite nun, co-Patron Saint of Europe, martyred at Auschwitz in 1941:

'Thy will be done,' in its full extent, must be the guideline for the Christian life. It must regulate the day from morning to evening, the course of the year and the entire life. Only then will it be the sole concern of the Christian. All other concerns the Lord takes over. This one alone, however, remains ours as long as we live... And, sooner or later, we begin to realise this. In the childhood of the spiritual life, when we have just begun to allow ourselves to be directed by God, then we must feel His guiding hand quite firmly and surely. But it doesn't always stay that way. Whoever belongs to Christ must go the whole way with Him. He must mature to adulthood: he must one day or other walk the way of the cross to Gethsemane and Golgotha.

Thérèse's Final Home - The Carmel

"Until my coming to Carmel I had never fathomed the depths of the treasures hidden in the Holy Face."

In April 1888, aged fifteen, Thérèse entered the Carmel at Lisieux, to lifelong enclosure within its walls, dedicated to serving the Lord through work, contemplation and prayer. "Everything thrilled me; I felt as though I was transported into a desert; our little cell, above all, filled me with joy … Ah! I was fully recompensed for all my trials. With what deep joy I repeated those words: 'I am here forever and ever!'" And these words were not just the romanticising of a teenager, for in her writing she reflects, "This happiness was not passing. It didn't take its flight with the 'illusions of the first days'. Illusions, God gave me the grace not to have *a single one* when entering Carmel. I found the religious life to be exactly as I had imagined it, no sacrifice astonished me, and yet, as you know dear Mother, my first steps met with more thorns than roses!"

The Carmel is close to the centre of town, quietly set back from the rue de Carmel. Just opposite is the town's helpful Tourist Information office, and a few yards down the street, the Lisieux Pilgrimage Information Office. Its contrast to the huge Basilica up on the hill could not be

The Carmel.

more stark, for it is here that the current community of Carmelite nuns quietly and prayerfully live out their vocation, and as pilgrims, we can have the privilege of joining them in this small, intimate chapel during their times of prayer.

Chapel

The chapel and chapel complex have recently been modernised and expanded, reflecting the Carmelite – and Thérèse's – life in a well presented, contemporary manner. Most importantly, though, it enables access to the focal point of your pilgrimage to Lisieux – the reliquary of St Thérèse. The whole frontage of the complex is enclosed by a tall glass and wood-panelled enclosure. The chapel's tall, pale, pillared and arched front façade greets you as you approach. To the right of the chapel is a reception centre and shop; to the left, across the small forecourt, a spacious indoor display area, the *parcours Thérèsien*, of which more, below.

Inside you will see a small, unadorned, simple liturgical church, displaying only the statues of St John of the Cross and St Teresa of Avila at the rear. It has a single nave, with chunky 'hit and miss', full length modern wooden panelling along the side walls. The same style panelling also backs the sanctuary, mounted on the central panel a simple carved wooden Corpus of the Crucified Christ. Solid, matching pews complete the harmony of the interior. The Sisters take their place in the choir at the front, and the congregation can join with them in their worship. It is a beautiful and serene experience, listening to their prayer and song, accompanied by the delicate plucking of a zither, played by one of the Sisters.

Meditation

By Mother Agnes of Jesus, Thérèse's elder sister, Pauline, a Carmelite Sister in the Lisieux Carmel between 1882 and 1951, and three times Prioress:

We must constantly listen to Our Lord, follow His inspirations, every day and every hour suffer what He permits, trust in Him for everything, and saying with our holy Little Thérèse: 'It is always what He does that I love'.

The Lord has told us in a prophecy that a sun of justice shall arise for those that love and there shall be healing in its rays.

The little drop of dew will not then be destroyed, but only drawn up and absorbed by the Sun of Love, and healing will be in its rays, that is to say, it will be absorbed and at the same time purified...

Let us think of Jesus only! Jesus! Oh, let us have only His Name and memory on our lips and in our hearts! We taste Heaven already when we love Him and accept His Cross. Suffering gives us the measure of His love for us, and in suffering we are assured of giving in return.

...As a delicate flower burned by the heat of the sun begs for dew to refresh it, thus your soul rises gasping to the heaven of Jesus' heart. And what will descend from that heart? Oh, ineffable mystery! Do not fear, in the shadow of the Cross there is refreshment and peace. More, there is a flood of love. Stay there, steeped in the Blood of Jesus... No hand can touch you, for if there is a virgin land it is there... the land one reaches through suffering, the land which for an instant raises us to the level of Jesus' Heart.

Reliquary

Off to the right of the chapel, and to all intents and purposes separate from it, is the semi-circular, domed side-chapel presenting St Thérèse's relics. In a large, ornate, glass-fronted reliquary (*chasse*), is the recumbent figure, fashioned in marble and precious wood, of Thérèse on her death bed. She lies peacefully, head tilted to the right, barefoot, clothed with the full Carmelite habit. On her head is a garland of white roses, and gently held to her breast with her left hand, is a crucifix; in her right hand, down by her side, she holds the rare golden papal rose presented by Pope Pius XI.

Above the reliquary, in a niche framed by one of the modern stained glass windows, is the original statue of the Virgin of the smile, which was in Thérèse's sick room at Les Buissonnets, and which was instrumental in her cure from serious illness. Flowers in abundance from the faithful are placed through the grille and laid in front of the reliquary. This whole peaceful scene radiates beauty and serenity; there is a small devotional area at the front where one can sit or kneel, and immerse oneself in this tranquil setting.

Prayer

Saint Thérèse,
Give us a simple, confident, loving and filial heart
turned toward Our Heavenly Father.
Help us to understand that faith, hope and love
are the whole of our life.

Show us that the Gospel
and our resemblance to Christ
are lived in our family, in our work
in our relations with our neighbour,
in the humble actions of our existence.

We entrust you to our weakness and our trials,
those of the little ones, the sick,
those victims of error, injustice and hatred.
Give us the strength to enlighten and rescue them.

And beyond our difficulties and our sufferings,
may the joy and peace of Jesus impregnate our life.
Amen.

The Carmel - Reliquary, and above, the statue of the 'Virgin of the smile'.

Sisters

Immediately off this side-chapel, where you see a statue of St Joseph, is another small viewing area. Here you can see the reliquary length-on, but if you glance through the full length window to your left you will see outside a simple tombstone, forming part of the side-chapel's wall, under which Thérèse's three Carmelite sisters are interred. On it is carved their names: 'La Révérende Mère Agnès de Jésus (Pauline) 1861 – 1951, Soeur Marie du Sacré-Coeur (Marie) 1860 – 1940, Soeur Geneviève de La Sainte Face (Céline) 1869 – 1959, Soeurs de la Sainte'. It is such a lovely thought that the mortal remains of these four Carmelite sisters in blood and in Christ remain close to each other in the Convent where they lived and prayed in close community.

The fifth – sometimes known as 'the forgotten sister' – Léonie, entered the Visitation Sisters' Convent, in nearby Caen, in 1899, taking the professed name of Sister Françoise-Thérèse. She is quoted as saying she had no regrets at not becoming a Carmelite, having, 'nothing but gratitude to God for having given me my Visitation vocation which I love.' She died in 1941 at her Convent, holding her sister Marie's rosary and Thérèse's profession crucifix.

Display

The *parcours Thérèsien* is a modern display area to the left of the chapel. In it, there are audiovisual displays of various aspects of life as a Carmelite nun. On the end wall, a large, projected video sequence gives a tantalising glimpse as the camera slowly sweeps round the Carmel cloister – the only view that the outside world is allowed – ending with a view slowly zooming in through the window of Thérèse's cell. Also on show are many artefacts of Thérèse and of her times in the Carmel – giving a fascinating insight to the life of enclosure during that period. There are some neat maps of Egypt drawn by Thérèse, Céline's bulky wooden box camera, through which many of the pictures of Thérèse were taken, the manuscript of Thérèse's production of Joan of Arc, as well as the costume she made for the play, complete with double-bladed sword.

Meditation

If you have time, before you leave this prayerful place, it might be worth quietly pondering these words from *Story of a Soul*, which perfectly sum up Thérèse:

How merciful is the way God has guided me. Never has he given me the desire for anything which he has not given me, and even his bitter chalice seemed delightful to me… Instead of doing me any harm, of making me vain, the gifts which God showered upon me (without my asking for them) drew me to him; and I saw that he alone was unchangeable, that he alone could fulfill my immense desires... I know that Jesus cannot desire useless sufferings for us, and that he would not inspire the longings I feel unless he wanted to grant them. Oh! How sweet is the way of Love! How I want to apply myself to doing the will of God always with the greatest self-surrender!... God cannot inspire unrealisable desires. I can, then, in spite of my littleness, aspire to holiness. It is impossible for me to grow up, and so I must bear with myself such as I am with all my imperfections... [The Lord] has always given me what I desire, or rather he has made me desire what he wants to give me... Your love [O my God] has gone before me, and it has grown with me, and now it is an abyss whose depths I cannot fathom... I ask Jesus to draw me into the flames of his love, to unite me so closely to him that he live and act in me. I feel that the more the fire of love burns within my heart, the more I shall say: 'Draw me'.

Final Thoughts

Contrasts

Having come to Lisieux you may be left with impressions, emotions and memories – some clear, some blurred, some unresolved – but at present they will be all about a person and a place, both, inextricably linked. In pilgrim terms, Lisieux is a place of contrasts: the mighty Basilica, which might be considered over-hagiographic, gaudy, and 'in-your-face', to the diminutive, gentle, humble Carmel, where today's Sisters live out their lives in the same obscurity and fidelity as Thérèse.

The Basilica, crammed, in gigantic scale with the overwhelming depiction of Thérèse's life and after-life – all of it designed by those who just wished to express that, in the most sincere, but explicit and glorious terms. It is a huge acknowledgement of her life and afterlife, and a desire to emphasise and perpetuate what she stands for, and in doing so, giving the thanks and glory to God. There is no doubting that it is a significant monument to a significant person.

Whether Thérèse approves or not is, of course, only conjecture. Her desire was to spend her 'Heaven doing good on earth' and taken in those terms, the Basilica is but an insignificant part of this global, universal mission

Eternal Peace.

of Thérèse – it is simply one of the many channels of
grace that imparts the Gospel message in its own
particular style. The Carmel, which expresses no more
than a simple, working church, that houses and
commemorates its most celebrated incumbent with such
great dignity and serenity, will continue ever on as just
that – a humble, working convent church – with the nuns
living out the Gospel life.

Reflections

So, in your reflections on these places, recalling the image
of that huge, glorious profusion of the Basilica, you can
give unrestrained and uninhibited thanks to God for
choosing and revealing Thérèse as one of His Mighty
Ones, and using her vocation of Love to such amazing
effect round the world. You might also like to pray for the
troubled nations of the world: those places that need peace
and understanding, and those that need missionaries to
spread the Gospel word.

In taking your thoughts back to the Carmel, and
dwelling on that sublime figure lying there so peacefully,
you can have a much more intimate conversation with
Thérèse herself, the person you may like to get to know
better. Here, you can thank God for His Hidden One, the
Humble One. You can ask her personally to help you live
by Love as she did, and to try and give your all to the little
things in life. In remembering her familial sisters that lie

close to her, you might also like to pray for vocations, for priests and for religious, particularly remembering the hidden ones in enclosure who, unseen, unknown and unheard by us, wholeheartedly devote their lives to praying for us. Remember also, those who are separated from family, for whatever reason, like Sister Françoise-Thérèse, Thérèse's sister, Léonie. Lastly, in remembering Thérèse's awful illness, you might like to pray for the sick and terminally ill – those known to you, and those not.

Then, in remembering that quiet, dignified cathedral in the town centre, you might like to pray for the Church in France, in the United Kingdom, and all the other parts of the world where the Church is beleaguered in some way. But you might also like to give thanks to all those parts of the world where the Church is burgeoning, currently Africa, India and South America.

In recalling Les Buissonnets, the Martin family home, you might like to pray for the sanctity of family life, to give strength and grace to your own family, and succour and comfort for those families who are broken and struggling. Pray for the abused. Pray also and particularly for young people, that they may look to this young person, who lived and died so heroically, as a role model.

For all of these places very strongly reflect Thérèse's message, and you can return to them in your mind, to keep you 'on message', and to give you visual support and structure when praying with Thérèse.

And then your reflections on Thérèse herself: coming to Lisieux might just have evoked your curiosity, maybe even a nascent admiration, despite maybe not having a great deal of prior knowledge about her. Well, you will not necessarily have to physically return to these places to get to know this self-effacing but steely personality better. This you can do by reading about her, reading her own writings, and most important, by praying with her, personally – and allow her to shower her roses on you. Then, you might begin to discover 'the breadth and length and height and depth' of what her life and thoughts may offer you in getting to know, and love, God more.

Finally, I leave you with an extract from a lovely poem of Thérèse – 'My Song for Today'. It is yours, too, for every day.

My Song for Today

My life is but an instant, a passing hour.
My life is but a day that escapes and that flies away.
Oh my God! You know that to love you on earth
I only have today!

If I think about tomorrow, I fear my fickleness.
I feel sadness and worry rising up in my heart.
But I'm willing, my God to accept trial and suffering
Just for today.

Ah! Lord, let me hide myself in your Face.
There I will no longer hear the world's vain noise.
Give me your love, keep me your grace
Just for today.

Near Your Divine Heart, I forget all passing things.
I no longer dread the fears of night.
Ah! Jesus, give me a place in Your Heart
Just for today.

O! Immaculate Virgin! You are my Sweet Star
Giving Jesus to me and uniting me to Him.
Oh Mother! Let me rest under your veil
Just for today.

(St Thérèse of Lisieux, extract from PN 5)

Other Places of St Thérèse

Lisieux

Church of St Jacques: prominent, handsome church building, which you will often pass on your to-ing and fro-ing between Basilica and other venues in the town. It dates back to 1540. It is no longer a consecrated church, but belongs to the municipal authorities, and is used generally as an exhibition venue, and occasionally for Thérèse-related displays.

Cemetery: About one kilometre on up past the Basilica. Location of the Martin family grave. Thérèse was initially buried here, as were her parents, Louis and Zélie, until their disinterment leading up to canonization, in Thérèse's instance, and beatification for Louis and Zélie. Thérèse's four brothers and sisters who died in infancy are also buried here: Marie-Hélène, Marie-Joseph Louis, Marie-Joseph Jean-Baptiste, Marie-Mélanie Thérèse. Thérèse's original grave is marked with her statue and a glass-encased wooden cross. Here also is the burial plot used by the Carmel, and the names of those closely involved with Thérèse's life at the Carmel are buried here – notably her Prioress, Mother Marie de Gonzague, and Sister Marie of the Angels, her novice mistress, as well as other Sisters of hers, and more recent, times. Their names can be seen at the foot of the statue.

More details about these places are available from the Lisieux Pilgrim Information Office, rue de Carmel.

Alençon

Alençon is Thérèse's place of birth, about 90 kilometres south of Lisieux. Family home (until the family left for Lisieux in 1877): 50, rue Saint-Blaise, open to the public.

Our Lady's Church: Church of Notre Dame, Grande Rue. The church in which Thérèse's parents were married, and Thérèse baptised.

Watchmaker and Jeweller's shop: 35, rue du Pont Neuf. The shop where Louis Martin carried out his business.

Further reading and Information

Websites:

www.therese-de-lisieux.cef.fr - Official Lisieux Pilgrim website.
www.thereseoflisieux.org - comprehensive website, with many links.

Reading

Story of a Soul, the Autobiography of St Thérèse of Lisieux, third edition, translated from the original manuscripts by John Clarke, OCD. ICS Publications, Washington DC, 1996.

CTS booklets on the life and spirituality of St Thérèse

Thérèse, teacher of Prayer, by Bro Craig (D 693)
The Message of Thérèse, by Vernon Johnson (D 331)
Thérèse of Lisieux, a biography, by Vernon Johnson (B 204)
The Little Way of Thérèse, In her own Words (D 707)
Louis and Zélie Martin, Parents of Thérèse of Lisieux, by Paulinus Redmond (B709)